Life Live

Life Live
March 2 - April 6, 2019

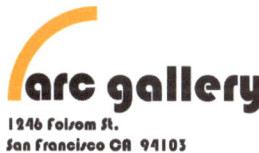

arc gallery
1246 Folsom St.
San Francisco CA 94103

Curator's Statement

The 9th Annual "Life Live" assembles five amazing practitioners of life drawing. Arc Fine Arts Consulting will be exhibiting their work in the Project Gallery. On Saturday, March 16th, the artists will be showcasing their skills "live" in figure drawing sessions open to the public in the main gallery. The gestural drawings will be ripped from their sketchbooks & displayed where they will be immediately for sale at $100 each.

Arc Fine Arts Consulting is established as a natural extension of the mission of Arc Gallery and Studios. Arc is dedicated to showcasing and promoting emerging and established artists in the San Francisco Bay Area. Here we are blessed with some of the most prestigious art schools in the country. On a per capita basis San Francisco boasts a higher percentage of working artists than any other city in the country. The opportunity for local collectors and businesses to build collections which tap into and support these communities is unparalleled. Arc Fine Arts is singularly dedicated to fostering those connections.

Curator:

Michael Yochum is a co-founder of Arc Gallery & Studios, along with Priscilla Otani, Stephen C. Wagner and former partner, Matthew Frederick.

Catalog designed by Michael Yochum
Arc Gallery © 2019

Featured Artists

Arlene Diehl

Diane Olivier

Eric Saint Georges

Allison Snopek

Jeremy Sutton

OPENING RECEPTION
Saturday, March 2nd, 7-9 PM

LIFE LIVE Live Drawing Event
Saturday, March 16th, 6:00-10 PM

CLOSING RECEPTION
Saturday, April 6th, 12-3 PM

Life Live

March 2 - April 6, 2019

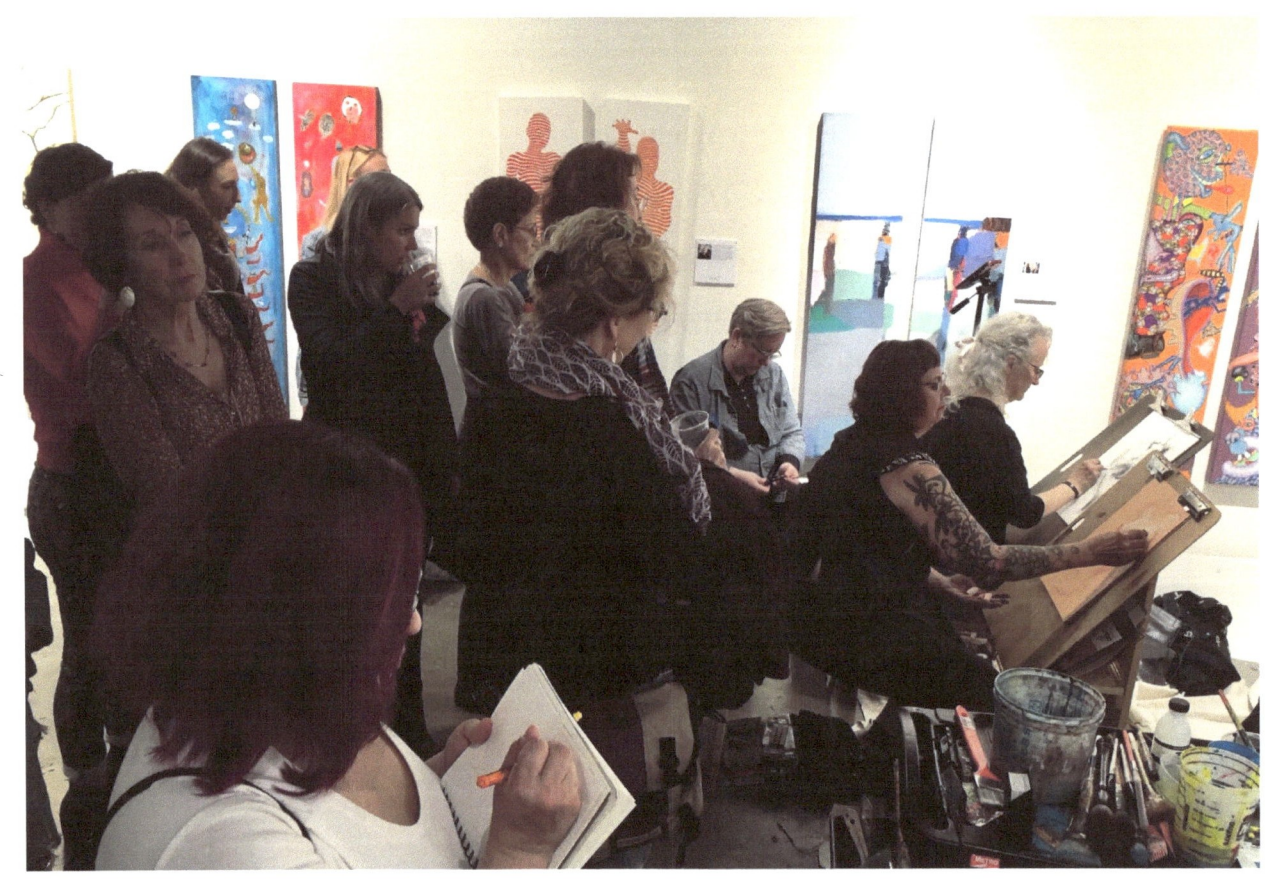

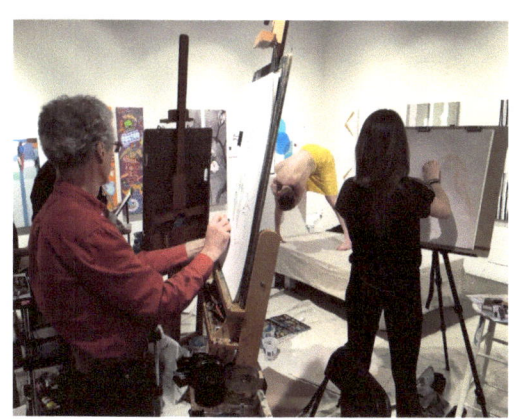
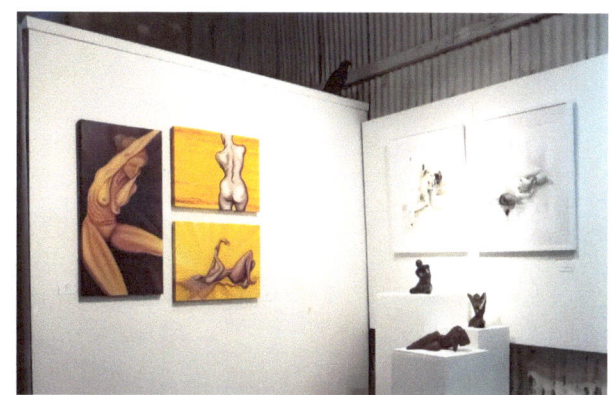
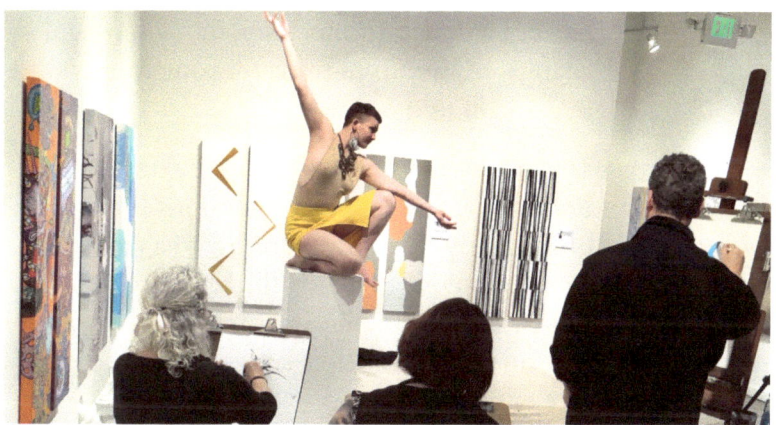
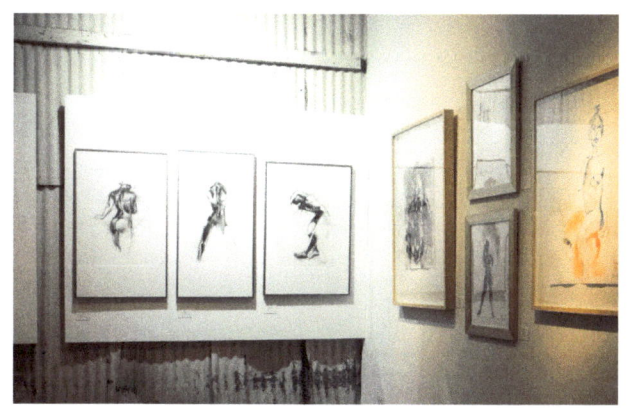
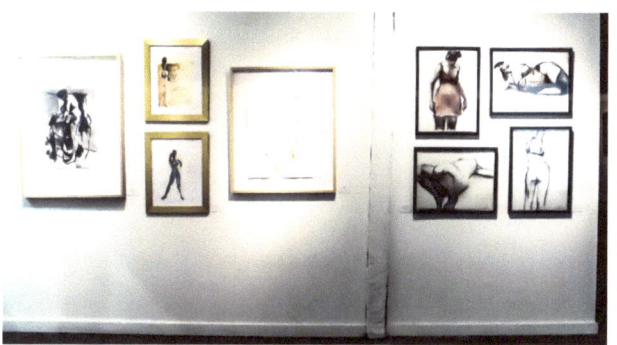

Arlene Diehl

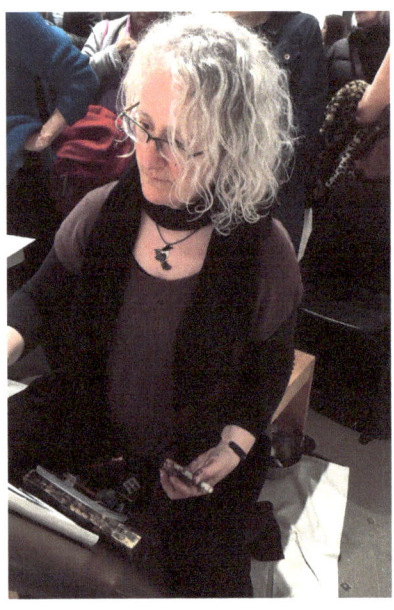

My work has evolved from a lifelong love for, fascination with, and sense of reverence for the human form. I have also been deeply committed over the years to the process of drawing, finding in it time and again an emotional and visceral immediacy that has served my deeper purposes. I am working now exclusively with live models and with a great deal of speed. I like working with a living, breathing human being because, by definition, the subject is not a static one but a dynamic one, moment by moment in a process of change. My aim is to transmit something of the power of that dynamism to the viewer.

This process requires of me a very deep letting off of the brakes of any preconceived notions I may have had for the drawing. By responding freshly to a particular moment the work can move in many different directions, sometimes more abstractly, sometimes more representationally. My best work often includes elements of both, and can be further layered with a sense of transition, emotional nuance and some measure of mystery.

website: https://www.artspan.org/artist/artistsartist
email: adiehl@sonic.net

ARLENE DIEHL was born in Massachusetts and raised in New England. Since 1990, she has lived here in San Francisco. She has exhibited her work continuously since her adolescence, in Boston, on Cape Cod, in the Bay Area, Los Angeles, Palm Desert, Australia and had her first solo show in Europe (July 2013); in the Netherlands.

EARLY RECOGNITION:

At 16, Arlene received the prestigious Strathmore Award in Drawing awarded annually to one high school student nationwide. (Exhibition/Competition N.Y. NY 1973) At 17, her self-portrait appeared on the cover of Senior Scholastic Magazine, her work was favorably noted in New York Magazine and she received a Merit Scholarship to Boston University School for the Arts(1974). She later transferred to the Boston Museum of Fine Arts School.(75-79)

SELECT SOLO EXHIBITIONS:

2013	*Mensielijk Lichaam (Human Bodies,* Gallery 0-68, Velp, The Netherlands
2012	*Drawings: Arlene Diehl*, Emac & Lawton PTY LTD, Botany, Australia
2006	*Figuration: Nineteen Drawings and One Bronze*, Anderson Smith North, San Rafael, CA
2004	*XY-zy: The Male Nude*, Klein's Exhibition Space, San Francisco, CA
2002	*Recent Drawings*, Reverie Gallery Cafe, San Francisco, CA
	Speaking Figuratively, Klein's Exhibition Space, San Francisco, CA

SELECT GROUP EXHIBITIONS:

2011-18	*Life Live I - VIII*, exhibition and live life drawing, Arc Gallery, San Francisco CA
2015	*The LGBT Show*, Linus Gallery, Los Angeles CA
2013	*Art Auction XV*, curated exhibition, Long Beach Museum of Art, Long Beach CA
2011	*The Figure Now*, Fontbonne University Fine Arts Gallery, St. Louis MO
2010	*Blake Collects: Living With Art*, Martha Bennett Gallery, Minneapolis MN
2008	*Articulating Art*, Left Coast Galleries, Studio City CA
	One Night Stand: Nude, Sensual and Erotic Work, ARTworkSF Gallery, San Francisco CA
2006	*Gestures In And On Paper: Original Works by Arlene Diehl, David Einstein and Minjung Kim,* Modern Masters Fine Art, Palm Desert, CA

COMMISSIONS: Arlene was commissioned to do a large (5 ft by 6 ½ ft.) charcoal drawing of ballroom dancers, interpreted from a 1950's Henri Cartier-Bresson photograph (1999) and also more recently to do a series of charcoal nudes of writer and poet Jewelle Gomez.

COMMUNITY::   Arlene is on the Board of Directors (and former acting president) of Red Umbrellas, a juried non-profit artists' exhibition group based in San Francisco.

PUBLICATIONS: Cover art: "Godin, held" by novelist Gustaf Peek (published in Dutch, 2014) Original drawings for "Tussen Malaise en Magie; Theater in het leven, Leven in het theater" 2011 Thomas de Neve (published in Dutch and German, 2012)

REPRESENTATION: Arlene is being represented by Art Gallery 0-68, in Velp, The Netherlands, Left Coast Galleries Studio City, CA., Rachelle Ryan Gallery Portland. OR, and by Emac & Lawton PTY LTD, Botany, AU

COLLECTIONS: Arlene's work is included in private collections across the United States and Canada, as well as in Great Britain, France, Germany, Ireland, Italy, Austria, The Netherlands, Hungary, New Zealand, Australia, Taiwan, Malaysia, The Philippines, Mexico, Honduras and Brazil.

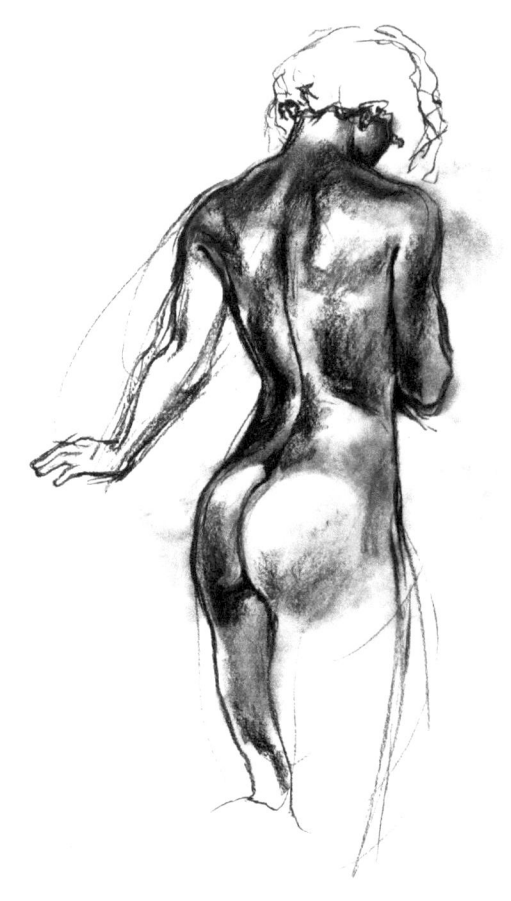

Untitled One
compressed charcoal on paper
36 1/4" x 22 3/4" $1150

Arlene Diehl

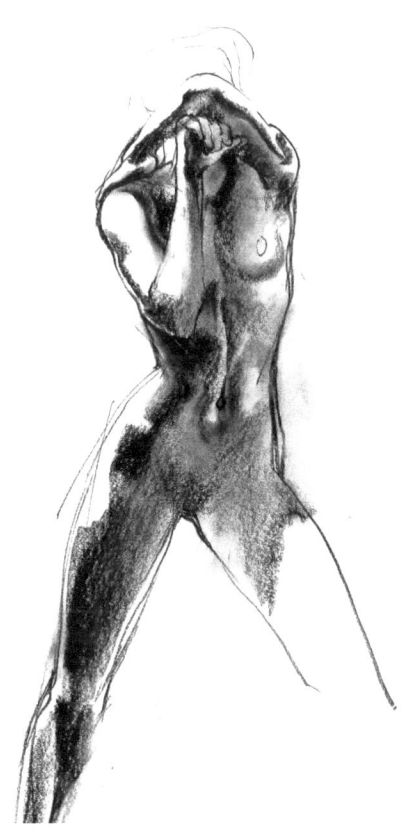

Untitled Two
compressed charcoal on paper
37 1/4" x 20 1/4" $1250

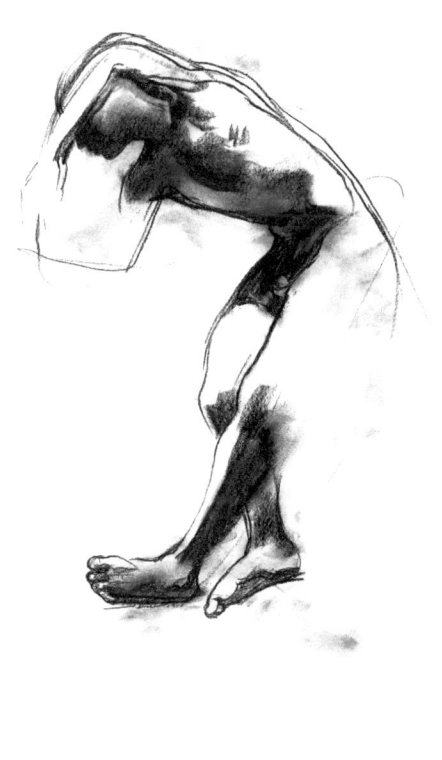

Untitled Three
compressed charcoal on paper
34 3/4" x 24" $1325

Arlene Diehl

Diane Olivier

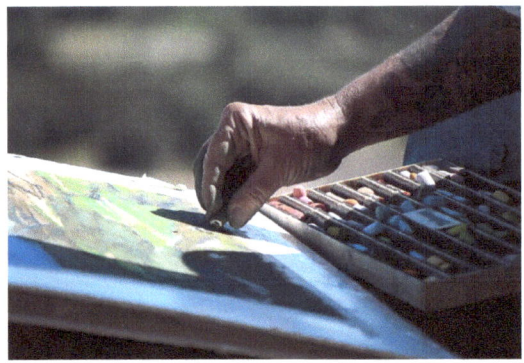

Drawing has always been my primary media, working with both traditional and nontraditional materials on scales ranging from small book size to mural size. My subjectmatter ranges from figurative, landscape and cityscapes to non-representational. The media ranges from charcoal to graphite, to full color pastels to non-traditional mixed media. The sense of touch between the tools and the paper and the immediacy of the mark are important element in my process. It is a dance between the eyes, the hand and the soul.

website: http://www.dianeolivier.com/
email: dianeolivier@me.com

Born in Rhode Island, Diane Olivier has been a resident since of California since 1990 and on full time staff at City College of San Francisco since 1991. She teaches Basic, Intermediate and Figure drawing every semester and hosts a series of drawing workshops abroad and in the U.S. each summer.

EDUCATION

1986	MFA University of California, Berkeley CA
1985	MA San Jose State University, San Jose CA
1978	BFA Rhode Island School of Design, Providence RI

SELECT SOLO EXHIBITIONS

1992	Dorothy Weiss Gallery, San Francisco CA
1990	Cabrillo College, Aptos CA

SELECT GROUP EXHIBITIONS

2018	*FourSquared*, Arc Gallery, San Francisco CA
2015	*LifeLive*, Arc Gallery, San Francisco CA
2014	*LifeLive*, Arc Gallery, San Francisco CA
2013	*LifeLive*, Arc Gallery, San Francisco CA
1990	*Drawing*, Palo Alto Art Center, Palo Alto CA
1989	*Selections 44*, Drawing Center, New York City, NY
1986	*Monumental Drawing*, Brooklyn Museum, Brooklyn NY
1988	*The National and International Studio Program Exhibition*, PS 1, Long Island City NY
1988	*Drawing*, San Francisco Arts Commission Gallery, San Francisco, CA
1987	*Drawing*, Richmond Art Center, Richmond CA
1987	*Awards in the Visual Arts*, Contemporary Art Center, Cincinnati OH

TEACHING

1991 -	City College of San Francisco, San Francisco CA
1990-91	San Jose State University, San Jose CA
1990	San Francisco Art Institute, San Francisco CA
1986 91	University of Cincinnati, Cincinnati OH
1984-86	Cabrillo College, Aptos CA
1983-84	San Jose State University, San Jose CA

ANNUAL WORKSHOPS - since 2000

South of France Drawing Workshop in the Languedoc
Morocco Drawing Workshop in Essaouira
Portugal Drawing Workshop in the Algarve
Gloucester Drawing Workshop in Massachusetts

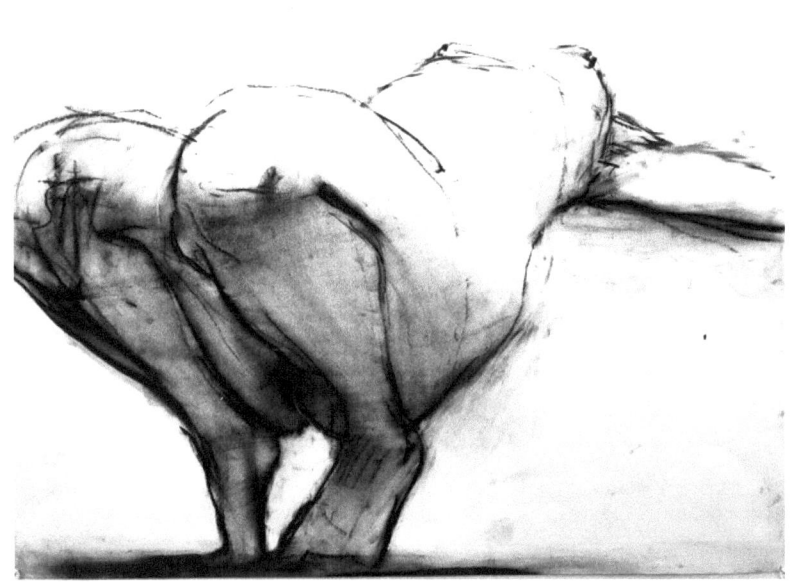

Muse 1: Prudence
charcoal on paper
18" x 24" $325

Muse 2: Diana
charcoal on paper
18" x 24" $325

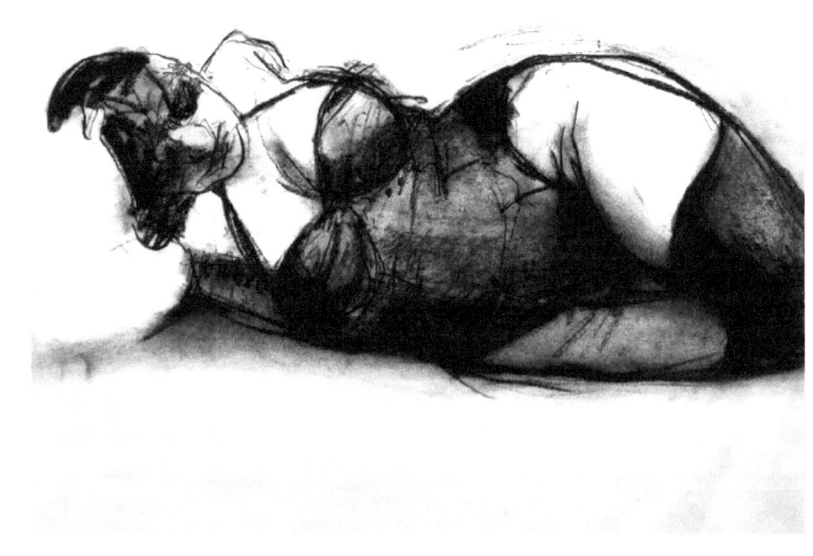

Diane Olivier

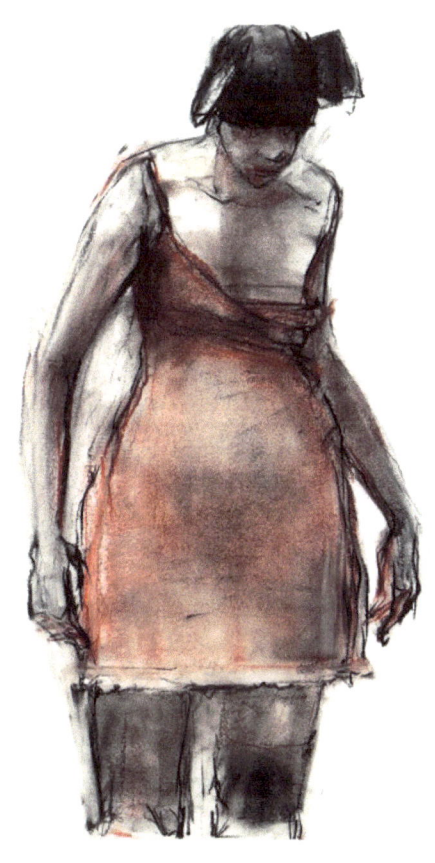

Muse 3: Cynthia
charcoal and pastel on paper
24" x 18" $325

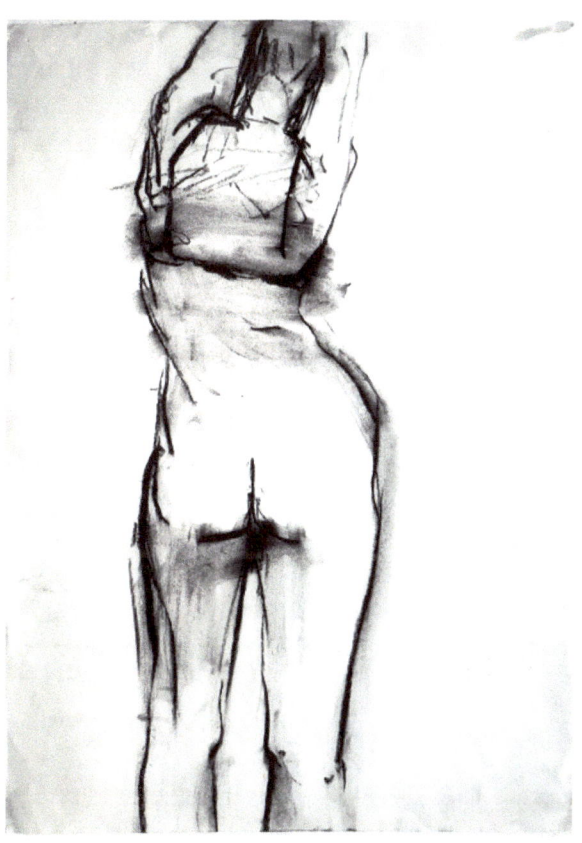

Muse 4: Jenny
charcoal on paper
24" x 18" $325

Diane Olivier

Eric Saint Georges

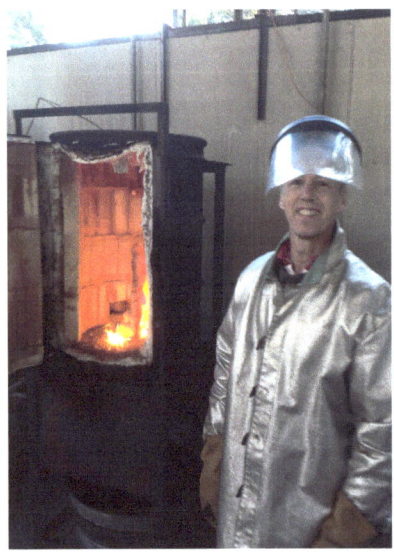

I watch the model, I feel the tension of her movement in my own body. With my knife I make bold cuts in the block of clay, trying to capture the essence of the pose. I have to work fast, to keep the energy flowing, and when I start to see some life emerging from the clay, I feel alive too...

I draw a few lines, quickly, sometimes with a couple of watercolor strokes. I do not think, just keep my focus on the model, enjoy the freedom of my hand moving, and the contact of the charcoal on the paper. Then, once in a while, the drawing is alive and I can feel the movement and the mood of the model, and I see that I have nothing to add to it and that if do, it is going to ruin it...

My main focus is on figurative sculpture and drawing. In my drawings I like to combine charcoal, ink and watercolor, which allow me to work quickly, my main interest being to capture life and energy in as spontaneous and raw a manner as possible. I draw almost exclusively from life, my preference being very short poses. I do not try to tell a story, as much as to capture the moment, the pose, the movement, themood. While I enjoy carving once a while a stone or a beautiful piece of wood, I create most of mysculptures in clay, either from life or from my life drawings. I then cast them in bronze, which is time consuming but very rewarding.

I spend now my time between my studio in Los Gatos (CA), various life drawing sessions in the Bay Area, the West Valley College foundry and teaching life drawing and sculpture. My longer term objective is to expand my art to other mediums, and to use my engineering background to combine art and technology.

website: http://www.ericsaintgeorges.com
email: contact@ericsaintgeorges.com

Born in Paris, France, ERIC SAINT GEORGES moved to the US in 1994.

As far as I can remember I have always been drawing and building things, but it is a workshop with the sculptor Petrus in 1978, which triggered my passion for sculpture. At that time, I had just completed my education in electrical engineering. Rather than going right away to work, I applied to the "Ecole Nationale Supérieure des Beaux Arts" in Paris, and studied drawing and sculpture there for 2 years, before spending several months with Petrus, from whom I learned the foundation of my clay technique. However, at the time, a career in art was not really an option for me (or so I thought) and I went back to pursuing a career as an engineer. Eventually, in 2015, after 35 years with limited artistic activity, I finally decided to go back to art full time.

SELECT EXHIBITIONS:

2018	*Life Live VIII*, exhibition and live life drawing, Arc Gallery, San Francisco CA
	Sculpture Now, Peninsula Museum, Burlingame CA (juried)
	Ruth Bancroft Sculpture Garden, Walnut Creek CA (juried)
	Human Form, Pacific Art League, Palo Alto CA (juried)
	stARTup Fair, San Francisco CA (juried)
	Work on Paper, Pacific Art League, Palo Alto CA (juried)
	Member Show, Pacific Art League, Palo Alto CA (juried, honorable mention)
2017	Ruth Bancroft Sculpture Garden, Walnut Creek CA (juried)
	Statewide 2D Competition, Triton Museum of Art, Santa Clara CA (juried)
	Gallery House, Palo Alto, CA
	Form of a Woman, Neologian Gallery, San Mateo CA (juried)
	Vyne Bistro, San Jose, CA
	Pacific Art League, Palo Alto CA (2nd Place)
2016	*Not so Heavy Metal II*, Mission College, San Jose CA (juried)
	More the Merrier, Art Ark Gallery, San Jose CA (juried)
	Instructor Exhibition, Pacific Art League, Palo Alto CA
	California Clay Competition, The Artery, Davis CA
	Figure and Faces, Pacific Art League, Palo Alto CA (juried)
	Art Object Gallery, San Jose CA (celebrating International Sculpture Day)
	Art Ark Gallery, San Jose CA (Silicon Valley Open Studio preview exhibition))
	Pacific Art League, Palo Alto CA
2015	Main St Cafe, Los Altos, CA
	Figure and Faces, Pacific Art League, Palo Alto CA (juried)

TEACHING:

2017 -	Instructor at Pacific Art League, Palo Alto CA (life drawing; figure sculpture)
	Teaching Assistant, Metal Sculpture, West Valley College, Saratoga CA

ART EDUCATION:

2015-16	Metal Sculpture at West Valley college (Saratoga) 2015-2016
1980-81	Resident with sculptor Petrus, France
1979-80	Ecole Nationale Supérieure des Beaux Arts, Paris, France. 1979-1980

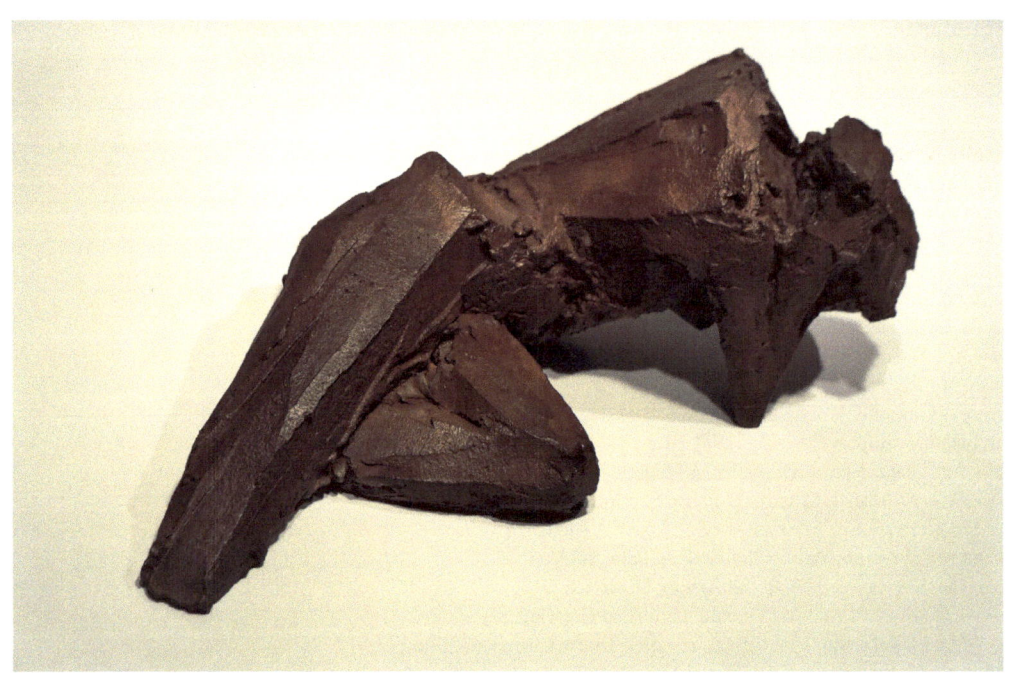

Becky Reclining
bronze
5" x 14" x 7" $2600

Eric Saint Georges

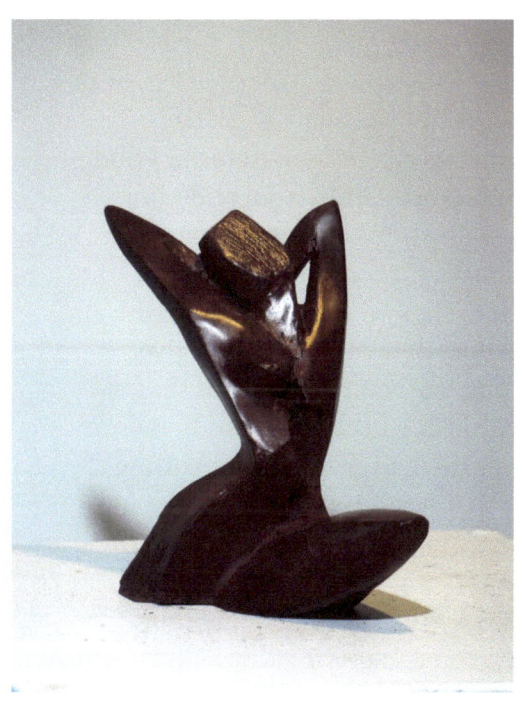

Morning Lady
bronze
8" x 6" x 4" $1400

Pearl
bronze
8" x 6" x 6" $1900

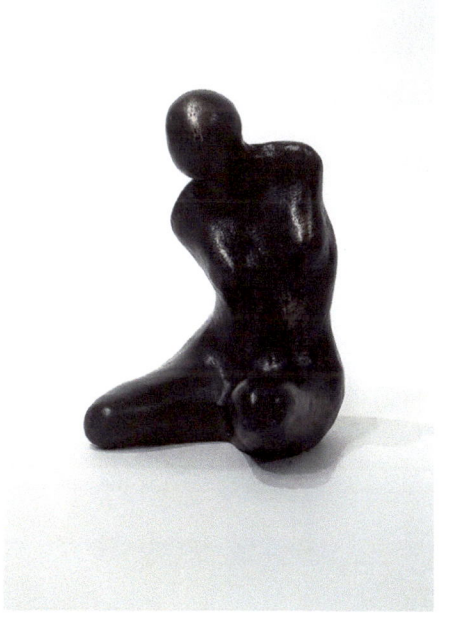

Eric Saint Georges

Allison Snopek

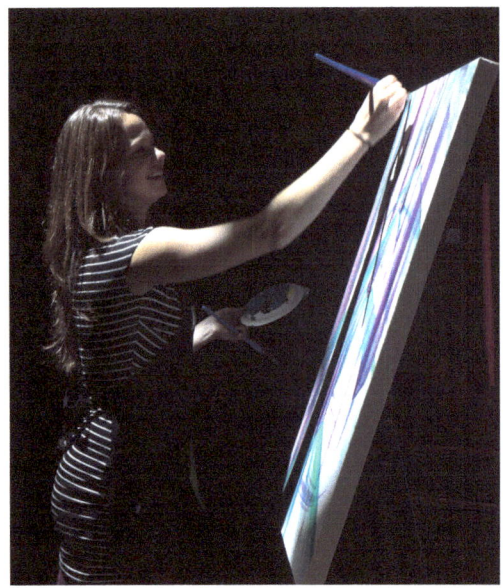

For the past several years, my work has focused primarily on the human form. I find inspiration and meditation from attending figure drawing sessions and exploring the expressive marks that convey gesture and emotion. Time slips away as I lose myself in the challenges of anatomy, perspective, foreshortening, curvature, light, and shadow. I take these drawing back to my studio where I ponder over them in search of something that evokes an interest in further developing, embellishing, and abstracting the figures. I transfer the drawings to canvas and begin a deliberate process of applying many thin layers of rich color, exploring the contrast and complements of color theory. The experience of painting becomes subconsciously expressive and transcendent, demonstrating the inner-workings of imagination and yielding vibrant representations of organic form.

website: http://www.allisonsnopek.com/
email: allison.snopek@gmail.com

ALLISON SNOPEK is an ever-evolving artist whose life and career have been intertwined with the San Francisco arts community since moving to the Bay Area in 2009. She works mainly with oil paint on canvas, from preliminary graphite and charcoal drawings on paper. In addition to this practice, she enjoys large-scale mural projects, sculpture, and community collaborations.

SELECT GROUP EXHIBIITIONS:

2018	City Art Cooperative Gallery, San Francisco, CA
2017	City Art Cooperative Gallery, San Francisco, CA
	Spring Spectrum. Hôtel Biron Wine Bar, San Francisco, CA
	Breasts: An Art Exhibit of Form and Function, The Public Works, San Francisco CA
	SFOS Hub Exhibition, The Mill Cafe, San Francisco, CA
2016	City Art Cooperative Gallery, San Francisco, CA
2015	City Art Cooperative Gallery, San Francisco, CA
2014	City Art Cooperative Gallery, San Francisco, CA

SOLO EXHIBITIONS:

2017	Swich Café, San Francisco, CA
2013	Secession Art & Design, San Francisco, CA
2010	Room Gallery, San Rafael, CA

OPEN STUDIOS:

2018	SF Open Studios at Asterisk Gallery, San Francisco, CA
2017	SF Open Studios at Mission Creek Park Pavilion, San Francisco, CA

LIVE PAINTING PERFORMANCE:

2017	*Daybreaker*, SOMArts Cultural Center, San Francisco, CA
	2 Blocks of Art Festival, San Francisco, CA
	Poetry in Parks, Candlestick Point State Recreation Area, San Francisco, CA
2016	2 Blocks of Art Festival, San Francisco, CA
	Poetry in Parks, Mt.Tamalpais, Mill Valley, CA
2015	*NightLife Gallery Crawl*, California Academy of Sciences, San Francisco, CA
2014	*Artbeats*, Pier 70, San Francisco, CA

MURAL PROJECTS:

2018	ArtSpan Hickory Alley Mural (Project Manager), San Francisco, CA
	ArtSpan Salesforce Transit Center Murals (Project Manager), San Francisco, CA
2015	ArtSpan Birdsong Mural (Project Manager), San Francisco, CA
2014	Undercover Presents Paul Simon's Graceland at Freight and Salvage, Berkeley, CA
2010	Italian Street Painting Festival, Community Action Marin, San Rafael, CA

TEACHING:

2013-14	Teaching Artist, SF Arts Education, San Francisco, CA
2013-14	Teaching Artist, Leap Arts in Education, San Francisco, CA

EDUCATION:

2008	BA Fine Arts, University of Minnesota, Minneapolis, MN

AWARDS:

2018	Art Enabler Award, Arts for a Better Bay Area, State of the Arts 2018

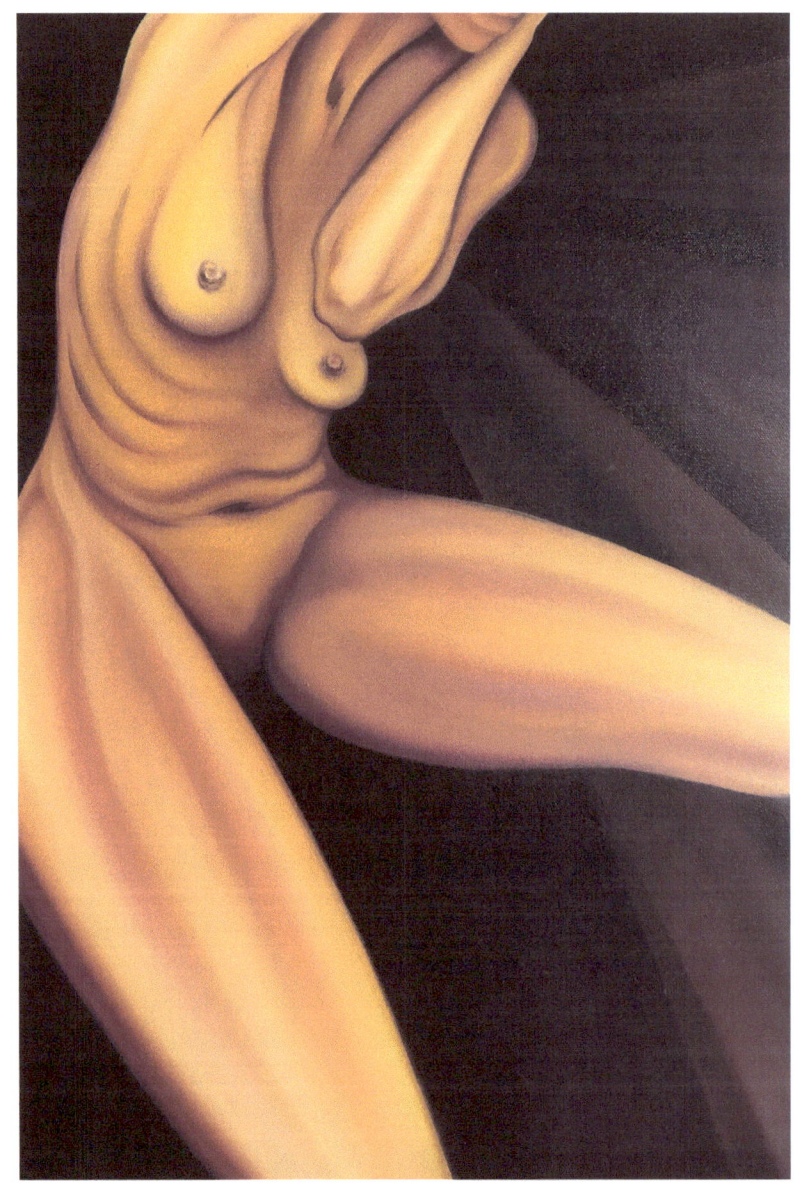

Imbroglio
oil on canvas
36" x 18" $795

Allison Snopek

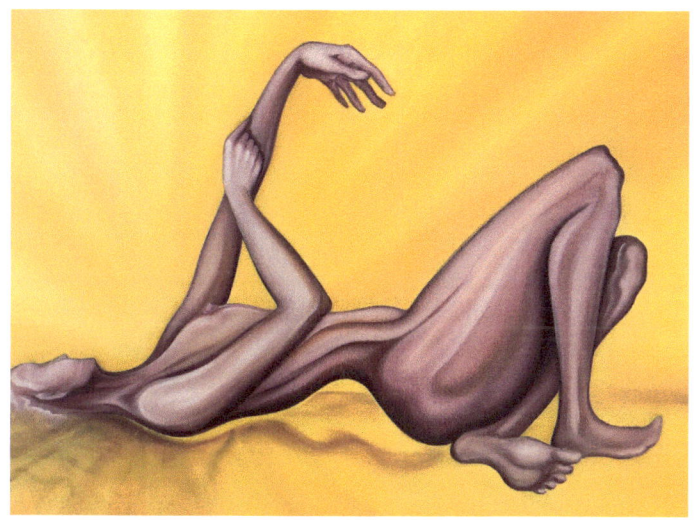

Afterglow
oil on canvas
18" x 24" $695

Torsion
oil on canvas
18" x 24" $695

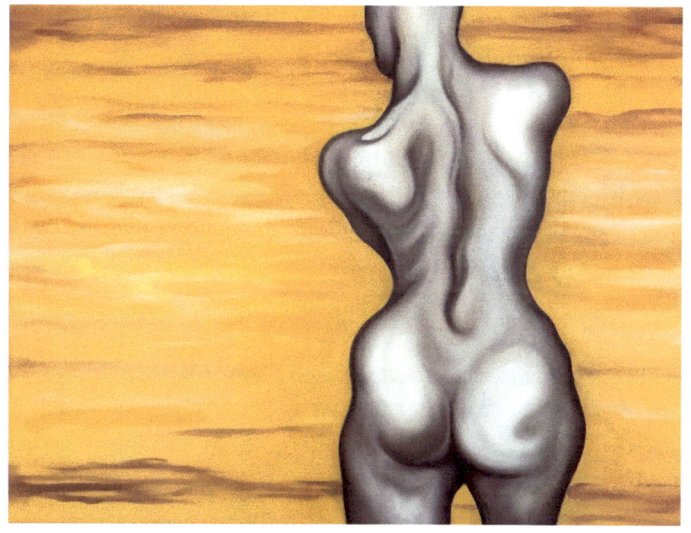

Allison Snopek

Jeremy Sutton

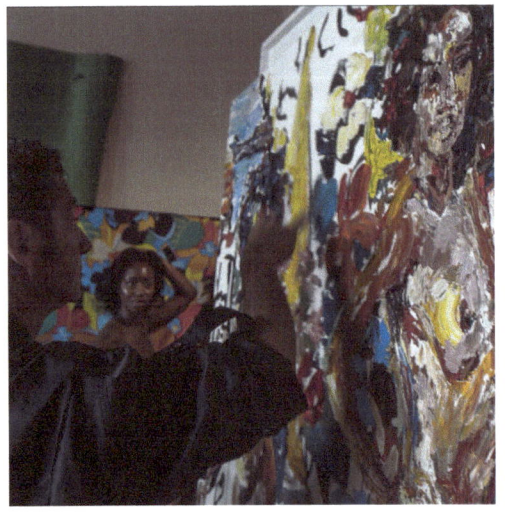

I was born in London, UK, and have drawn since I was three. I studied physics at Oxford and pursued a first career selling superconducting magnets and cryogenic research systems around the world, a career which led me to move to the heart of Silicon Valley in 1988. It was there that I was introduced to digital painting in 1991 and changed my career from physics to art in 1994.

Drawing the figure from life has been the foundation of my art for many decades, from the life drawing classes I took at the Ruskin School of Drawing & Fine Art, Oxford University, whilst studying for my Physics degree; through life drawing at the Vrije Academie in The Hague, the Netherlands, where I lived in the mid-1980s; to the sessions I attend at Fort Mason and Sharon Art Studio and other places locally, and host at 1890 Bryant Studios. Over a professional art career spanning twenty-five years and specializing in digital media, I still love to draw the human figure from life with traditional media on paper.

There is no substitute for the liveliness, dynamism and energy of the collaborative creative experience in drawing from life—every moment offers a slightly changed point of view with slightly different lighting, angles and perspective. The model's energy and attitude feed into the drawer's creation, and vice versa: the drawer's energy feeds into the model's. The life drawing process is a circle of shared energy and inspiration!

As a live event painter working on the iPad, as well as with traditional media, I utilize the skills developed from the quick gesture poses of life drawing, where you have to capture the essence in a few lines. Live painting on stage with Tommy Igoe's Birdland All-Stars' Art of Jazz east coast tour (20 cities in 5 weeks), I put that gesture drawing experience to good use, painting the musicians who were in constant motion.

website: https://jeremysutton.com/
email: jeremy@jeremysutton.com

EDUCATION

1982 MA Oxon (Physics), Pembroke College, Oxford University, UK
1980-82 Drawing, Sculpture & Print-Making, Ruskin School, Oxford University, UK
1985-88 Lithography & Drawing, Vrije Academie, The Hague, NL

SELECTED HONORS

2005- Corel Painter Master Elite

SELECTED PUBLIC ART COMMISSIONS

2014 Silicon Valley Series, eight 60" x 60" prints on aluminum, San Jose Marriott, San Jose CA
2011 *Classic San Francisco*, Large Heart, part of the Heroes & Hearts Fundraising Campaign, San Francisco CA

SELECTED ONE PERSON EXHIBITIONS

2019 *Endless Dance*, Embarcadero Conference Center, San Francisco CA
2006 *San Francisco Bay Area Women of Style*, Nordstrom, San Francisco CA
1993 *Holocaust Survivor Portraits*, Berkeley-Richmond Jewish Community Center, Berkeley CA
1989 *Faces*, Gordon Biersch, Palo Alto CA

SELECTED GROUP EXHIBITIONS

2017 *iPad Art: Places – 3 Brits in Silicon Valley,* Art Ventures Gallery, Menlo Park CA
2015 *DigiFun Art: Urban Scape Mobile Art Exhibition & Festival*, Seoul Museum of Art, Seoul, Korea
2005 *More Than a Game: The Art of Baseball*, George Krevsky Gallery, San Francisco CA
1995 *Art & Technology*, The Tech Museum of Innovation, San Jose CA
1993 *Breaking Down Walls*, Ansel Adams Center, San Francisco CA
1990 *Self-Portraits*, Syntex Gallery, Palo Alto CA

SELECTED LIVE EVENT PAINTING

2018 *Art of Jazz East Coast Tour*, Birdland All-Stars featuring Tommy Igoe
2015 *America Now! Innovation in Art*, Smithsonian American Art Museum, Washington, DC
2014 Nuit Blanche Arts Festival, Toronto, Canada
2013 *David Hockney Bigger Exhibition*, de Young Museum, San Francisco CA
2011 *Totem*, Cirque du Soleil, San Francisco CA
1995 TED Conference, Monterey CA
1994 Virgin Atlantic San Francisco Inaugural, San Francisco CA

SELECTED PUBLICATIONS

2004-09 Painter Creativity: Digital Artist's Handbook, Focal Press

SELECTED WORKSHOPS / TEACHING

2015 iPad Sketching Workshop, Victoria & Albert Museum, London, UK
2014-17 Mobile Digital Art & Creativity Summit, Palo Alto & Mountain View CA
1996 Academy of Art University, San Francisco CA

SELECTED SPEAKING ENGAGEMENTS

2017 Portrait of a Risk-Taker: An Artist's Risk Management Journey, Philadelphia PA
2015 Hands On! Conference, Rijksmuseum, Amsterdam, The Netherlands
2013 Painting in 3D Space, Moses Znaimer's ideacity Conference, Toronto, Canada
2008 Macworld, San Francisco CA

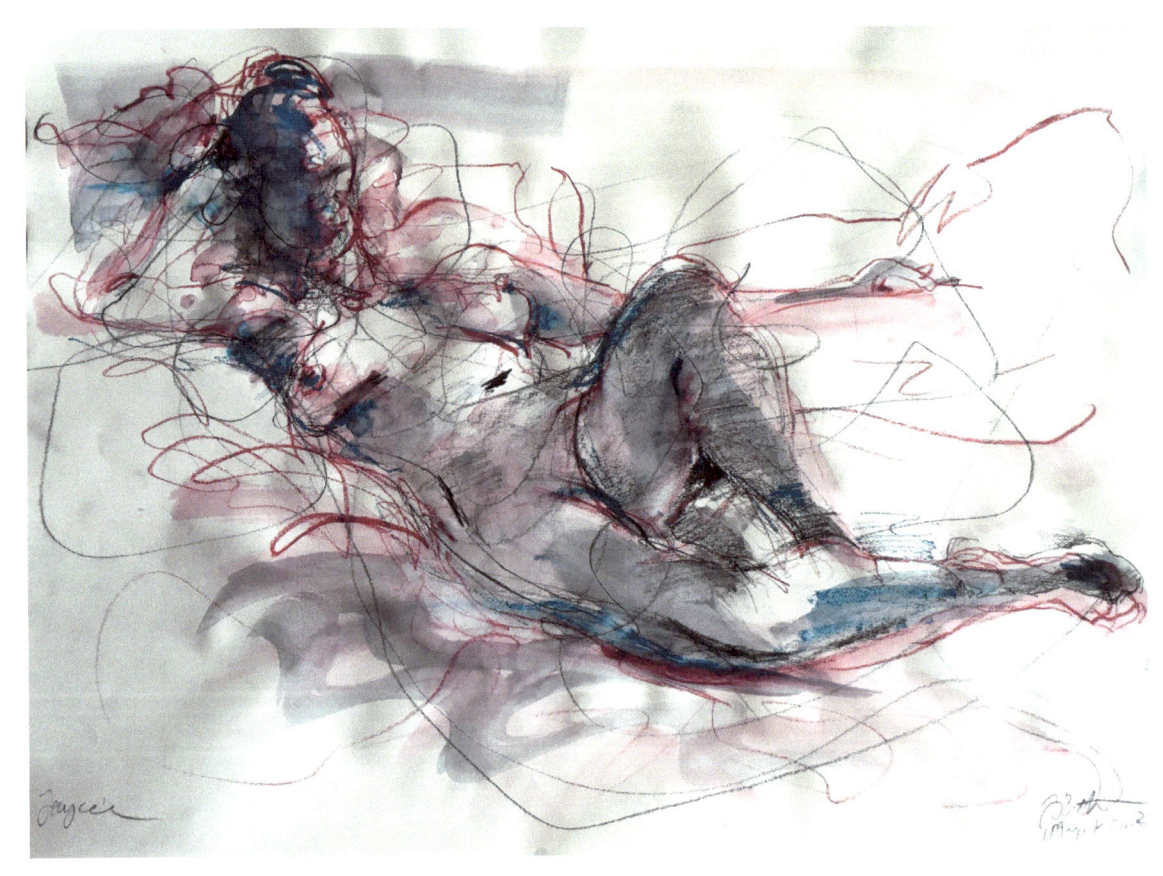

Jaycee
crayon and graphite on paper
16.5" x 23.5" $2200

Jeremy Sutton

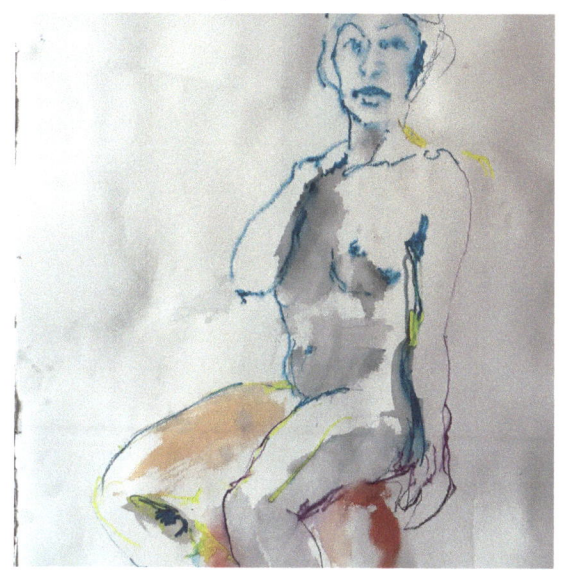

Laurel Sitting
acrylic on canvas
27" x 22" $950

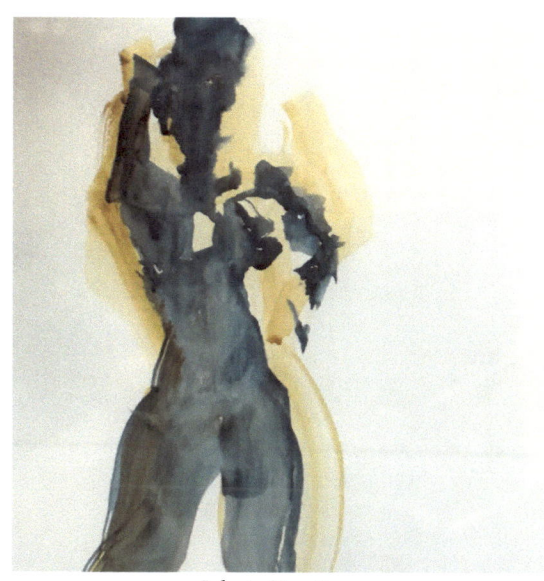

Inky in Two Tone
acrylic on canvas
16" x 12" $750

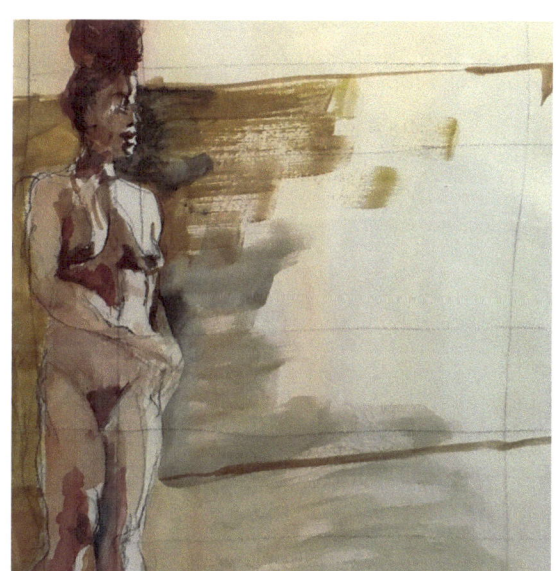

Inky in Sepia
acrylic on canvas
16" x 12" $750

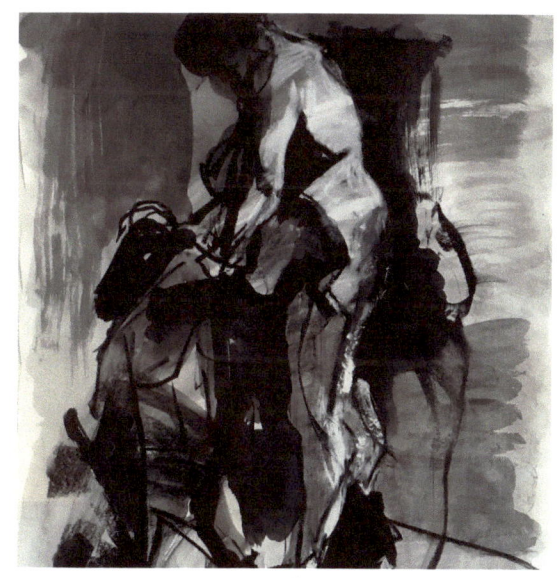

Diana Looks Down
acrylic on canvas
17.5" x 23.5" $1200

Jeremy Sutton

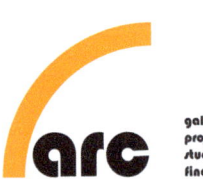

gallery
project gallery
studios
fine art consulting

1246 Folsom St.
San Francisco, CA

http://arc-sf.com
http://arcfinearts-sf.com
arcgallerysf@gmail.com
415-298-7969

www.ingramcontent.com/pod-product-compliance
Lightning Source LLC
Chambersburg PA
CBHW051832210526
45473CB00005B/1838